Coming Out
of the Dark

Coming Out of the Dark

Aisha Night

authorHOUSE®

AuthorHouse™
1663 Liberty Drive
Bloomington, IN 47403
www.authorhouse.com
Phone: 833-262-8899

Published by AuthorHouse 08/24/2020

ISBN: 978-1-4969-5600-2 (sc)
ISBN: 978-1-4969-5601-9 (e)

Print information available on the last page.

This book is printed on acid-free paper.

CONTENTS

INTRODUCTION

My name is Aisha Night.

It took me some time to decide whether I should write this book. I was thinking about the embarrassment it would bring to me and my family. But I thought this book could help someone who may be or has been going through similar situations in life. I decided to tell the world how I overcame what happened in my life and how God blessed me so that I am still here today.

I thank my entire family for their support in my time of need. I especially thank my sisters. We have experienced a lot of hard times, good times, and lots of tears, all which have shaped us to be strong women of God, positive mothers, and loving human beings.

Although I may not tell my family how I feel very often, I want them to know that I love them with every fiber of my being. I also want to thank my brothers for always putting up with me no matter what. I believe that when you have a loving family, you should hold on to the memories, whether good or bad, because at the end of the day, that's all we really have.

I thank my mom for always dealing with my father's crap and for staying strong, trying to raise us the right way. The following words are from my heart: I pray you have a blessed life. Your prayers are heard.

Grandma, thank you for keeping our family together. Even though you know that most of us don't have a relationship with God, no matter how many times we have messed up, you have never given up on us. Love you.

Father God, thank you for giving me the strength and courage to write this book!

CHAPTER ONE

When I was living with my grandmother, things weren't so bad. My grandmother used to make sure we had food, clean clothes, heat, and hot water. There came a time when my grandmother had to move on with her life because all of her children were grown. She had seven children. She was a strong woman of God who continually prayed for her family.

I remember sitting around and talking about how the family had expanded from two people. My grandmother and her sister started what years later turned out to be a mess. Between the two of them, they had fourteen kids.

After my grandmother moved on, my mom became the owner of her house. Lots of things changed, and it seemed always to be cold. I remember the hunger pains from not eating every day and night. I can still hear my siblings crying because they were either hungry or cold.

Our house was in need of so many repairs that we played in it as if it was some type of clubhouse.

We shared beds because it was the only way to stay warm. Most of the time, we would be afraid to fall asleep because we had huge rats running around. The rats were almost as big as the cat we owned. At night we could hear the rats chewing through the walls. Our cat would try to catch them before they could reach the steps, and the fights between the cat and rats were extremely loud. There wasn't a morning my mother wouldn't have to clean up the remains of the rats that the cat had left behind.

It seemed to me that anybody was allowed to move in. If you needed a place to stay, our house was the house to come to because the doors were always open.

You see, my mother was mentally ill. People in her life were very much aware that she did not know how to make good decisions, so they always took advantage of her. When we were hungry, my mother would pay the people who stayed with us so we could eat. Sometimes they would make us work just for a plate of food.

It wasn't long before people began selling drugs and running in and out to stash drugs. School began to get less and less interesting to us because there was too much going on at home to worry about. There was constant drinking, and fights broke out every day as if it was a boxing ring. There were so many things going on at our house that any kid would have been confused. As a child, I always wanted to confront my mom and ask her why she allowed other people to come to our house and do whatever they wanted whenever they wanted to do it. It's not like any of them helped to raise us or gave support. I often wondered why she allowed everybody to run all over her. My mother was always getting beat up on, cussed out, and sometimes kicked out of her own house.

Shortly after I had my first child at the age of sixteen, it became too much for us all. That was the worst day of my life! We finally spoke up and told her to stop putting up with people's abuse. We demanded that she shut down that house and move into another. Then maybe all those other people would move on with their lives.

My parents didn't have a problem cussing us out. They told us that if we didn't like the things that were going on there, we could get the hell out. There were several days when I would just pack my baby bag and try to get away from that house. I took the baby and walked the streets all night long until the buses started running, not knowing where to go. I thought I had everything all planned out, but I knew nothing at that age.

I thought surviving without going back home would be easy, but I had no clue how to live on my own with my baby, even though I never stopped trying to survive. So I stayed at the house of some friends for about two weeks. That was short-lived because they really didn't have a place for my baby and me to sleep. My mom continued receiving money from welfare on our behalf, but she refused to give me money to pay rent, and it was difficult for me to take care of myself and my child. Jeffrey, my baby's father, didn't stick around much, mostly because he was six years older. But the flip side was that I never wanted younger boys because they were too immature. Also, they were too young to get a job and help support me.

I learned at an early age that I was attracted to older men. Most of the men I dated were much older than I was. I had some friends who came and went, but just this one was very special to me. We began a long-term relationship. At that time, no one could tell me anything negative about Jeffrey, even if it was true.

I think his age played a huge part in my falling in love with him. He already was experienced in relationships, and he seemed to know just how to treat a woman. He was so soft-spoken. There was nothing that I couldn't tell him because he always had a listening ear.

He gained my trust and captured my heart. It took only four months to get pregnant by him. I still lived with my parents in that hellhole of a house. At the time, Jeffrey was able to get groceries, Pampers, and milk on credit. He repaid his debt every time he got paid. He helped as much as he could with obtaining things for our child. One day, I told him to move in with me so he could help with some of the bills. At the time, I was only fifteen years old, and he was twenty-one. If my parents hadn't been so desperate for money, I believe they never would have allowed him to move in with us. He paid rent every month.

After a while, things started getting out of hand. People started turning against me. I would hear them on many occasions talking about how they wanted me and Jeffrey out the house. I couldn't understand because Jeffrey paid his way. Most of the put-downs came when the refrigerator was low. Everyone would always get mad when Jeffrey came home with food only for me, him, and our child.

I always felt like the black sheep of the family. Problems were never resolved. I decided to do what was best for me: leave! I didn't think anyone would actually miss us. I got to a place where I demanded that Jeffrey stop paying rent. When I decided to leave, there were all kinds of problems because I was still a minor and my baby and I were under the care of a legal guardian. I wanted to leave so badly that I gave my child to my parents.

When I moved out with Jeffrey, things got worse instead of better. I began to run the streets all the time and at any time of night. Jeffrey never got around to asking his mom if I could stay, so we used to wait until she fell asleep and then sneak into the house. We had no choice some nights but to sleep anyplace out on the streets or sometimes in stolen cars. In my ignorance, I didn't care who saw me naked when I woke up. To me, this was fun. But once in a while, I would stop and think about my child. Running the streets got to be tiring, but because I wanted to be with Jeffrey, I never told him. It was crazy because every night we had to find someplace to sleep. Jeffery's parents put him out because of his stealing habit. I wanted to go back home, but my parents were living together again. I just could not bear to live with them with the physical and verbal abuse.

In time, I got pregnant with my second child. When Jeffrey's parents heard about my pregnancy, they allowed us back in the house. We were on watch while we stayed with them because of his stealing. No one trusted him.

Eventually I found out Jeffrey was on drugs and couldn't control his habit. When Grandma gave me money to spend, Jeffrey never hesitated to ask for twenty dollars. I often wondered what he was doing with the money I would give him, but I never asked. I noticed he would spend a lot of time at friends' houses. He claimed they were only smoking marijuana.

I constantly accused him of sleeping with other women. We fought often because I thought he preferred someone his own age. There were many times I couldn't hold a conversation with his friends because I was too young. We fought all the time, and I needed someone to help raise my children. Jeffrey's parents informed me that we would have to leave because things were coming up missing.

So I moved back with my parents until my daughter was born. Here I was, a teenager with two children only nine months apart. I tried to return to school and was glad I did. I felt like I was more than just a mother when I was in school. I couldn't wait until I got home to see my babies. I felt like a business woman, except I didn't have a job.

Going back to school worked out well. Mom took care of my children for me. Suddenly, Jeffrey began to call and ask about the kids. He told me that he had a new place to stay, and he didn't miss the opportunity to say that he missed me and the girls. He apologized for fighting and claimed he wasn't using drugs any more. Needless to say, I allowed him back into my life because I didn't want to be a single mom. When I began spending nights with him, the nights became weekends. That was the end of school. I missed so many days that I just didn't go back.

I moved in with Jeffrey at his new house and later learned that wasn't a wise decision. I had my own welfare check and thought I was grown. I enjoyed showing Jeffery I was grown and could now do grown-up things. I began to go food shopping and cooked for everyone in the house. But for some reason we were running short on food. My guess was that someone was taking food out of the house to sell for drugs, so I had to call around plenty of times to borrow money for food. That didn't work for long, either, because people got tired of me asking. So they told me to tell my man to get a job and take care of his family.

The last time Jeffery worked was at the market. After that he had no job. He thought because he helped me get welfare, I was his job. Each time I got my check, he had his hand out.

It got so bad that I began to lie about having money. But he was slick. He waited until I went to bed and checked my pants or looked under the bed for it. He would steal money from me and my children and share it with others for drugs. There were times when he would check all over the house for my money. My children were in need of Pampers and milk, but that didn't stop him.

Jeffrey would even go so far as trying to have sex with me for money. Isn't that crazy? He thought if he was nice and sweet to me I would do anything for him. Having sex with him made me so sick that I would run to the shower when he was done. I felt so nasty that I would scrub for hours in the shower because I felt I was being raped. He would climb on top of me and have his way.

There were days we walked miles just to eat dinner at someone else's house because we didn't have any money for food. One day my baby didn't have any Pampers, so we used a maxi-pad as a diaper, kept together with plastic tied on both sides.

When I thought things couldn't get any worse, the fights started again. Whenever it was time for me to visit my family, Jeffrey would want me to ask for money, or he would want me to pay him just for going out. If I couldn't give him money, he would try to stop me from visiting. He would often take the children away from me and then tell me I could go without them, just to make sure I was coming back.

He had total control over me. I was told what and what not to eat and what time to eat. People would try to intervene and tell him to stop treating me like a child. He controlled my eating habits because he didn't want me to gain weight. My self-esteem was already low, because whenever he was upset with me all I ever heard was how fat I was and how bad I looked. I knew in my heart that what we had was over, but I just didn't know how to get out of it. My family meant everything to me. I began to have flashbacks of how he used to climb on top of me and have sex when I wasn't in the mood. That made me sick.

There were times when my children didn't get anything for Christmas or birthdays because he stole and sold their gifts. My children had hunger pains when they didn't have anything to eat all day. There were times when Jeffrey searched the entire house, looking for money that I put away for the next day. I remember the nights when I would take a shower and just cry because I didn't know how to get myself out of this horrible relationship.

The worst thing was feeling trapped by someone who was six years older than I. There was never a time when I could go out alone or with a friend and just do things like any other teenager. I had to be in his presence constantly to make him feel secure. This is how he got his power to control everything I said or did.

CHAPTER TWO

I had my third child and was living in a one-bedroom apartment. It was so crowded that I had no room to move around. Most of the time I had to remove my children from the house just so they could have a place to play and run around. But as much as I wanted to take my children somewhere nice, I couldn't because I had no money to spend. I was depressed because I never got to go shopping for my children or hang out with any of my siblings. I was left sitting in a room, not doing anything with my life, and having children with this person who was a sorry excuse for a man.

I tried many times to leave him, but no one would put up with me because of Jeffrey. Nobody liked him because of the way he treated me and the kids. I stopped trying to leave him and tried to make it work. Whatever it was that I needed to do, I just went ahead and did it.

In the meantime, he never knew that I was saving money to move out. I kept thinking that if we could get our own place, things would work out better for us. Here we were, stuck in this little room where we couldn't even move around, with nowhere for the kids to play or even sleep.

At that time, I was happy because I was thinking that Jeffrey finally came to his senses and wanted to do right for his family. He even started getting up every day and looking for a job, but that didn't last long. Within a week's time he had given up on looking, but he never told me anything. All I knew was he used to come in the house with around thirty dollars, saying that he did little odd jobs for people, and that's how he got the money. I didn't care where the money came from just as long as it wasn't from me. One day he gave me the thirty dollars to put up with the rest of the money I had already. The funny part was he made sure that he kept at least twenty dollars for himself so that he could by his drugs. It was party time for him because he had money.

My kids and I just sat in that room, smelling that smoke coming from underneath the door. All night he would beg me for money. I agreed to loan it to him. Then maybe I would get it back like he said. But why did I do that? The party lasted all night. Smoke was all over the house.

He looked like a mummy to me. I couldn't stay awake any longer to watch my money go up in smoke. When people take drugs, you never know what they're capable of. I was scared for myself and my children. Also, I didn't want Jeffrey to steal my money. That's the real reason I couldn't sleep. But I fell asleep anyway, and every dime I had saved was stolen. I tried to lie on top of my money so if he did try to steal it, I would feel him moving me over. That didn't work. I can't explain all the times I tried to find ways to keep money from him so we could live a better life in our own home. I watched my dreams go up in smoke.

I knew I had to make a move somehow without Jeffrey being in our life. The scary thing was I didn't even know where to go because I'd been tagging with him since I was fifteen years old. Where would I start? What steps would I have to take for me and my children to be comfortable and safe? When Jeffery went out of the house, even though I didn't know where he was going, I quickly got up and started packing for me and my children. I moved around the room so fast and had so many bags in my hands, I almost forgot my third child. After I finished packing, I called a friend to come pick us up. It was like a breath of fresh air.

As we started driving away, my friend asked me what happened and whether we were fighting. I said no, we were not fighting. I just wanted to get out of the house to spend some time with her. She believed it at the time. I never said a word about my kids and me not having a place to go. I just made up a lie about going to a relative's house. Part of me was hoping that once I arrived at my destination, maybe my kids and I could stay over—and if I couldn't, then just my kids.

But it didn't happen that way. At my relative's house I just sat around, trying to wait until everyone was asleep so my kids and I could stay over. For some reason they kept coming downstairs to check on us to see if we had left yet. Meanwhile, my kids were getting sleepy, the time was getting later and later, and we still didn't have a place to go. People kept coming downstairs to see if we had left yet. I overheard someone say that all the doors needed to be locked and all company needed to go home. When I asked if we could stay over, the answer was no, so I couldn't do anything but leave.

Before I left, I asked what was going on. If I can't stay, I asked, could they keep my kids? I really didn't care where I was going to stay and sleep as long as my children were safe. That's all that mattered to me. That night when I left the house, I was hurt because I had to leave my kids. They were all that made me happy. It was a bittersweet feeling because at least my kids didn't have to walk the streets with me all night.

As I walked the streets, something happened to me. I didn't realize it until I got outside and started walking around and crying. I didn't know where to go and what to do. By then it was very late. No wind was blowing, and it was just right outside. It was as if God knew that I was out there. As I was walking, I could see all the stars in the sky. At that moment I stopped being afraid of being outside so late by myself. I felt as if I had someone walking with me, and I just started talking to God about my problems. Tears were coming down my face as I asked God what I should do about my kids. I asked him to give me a place to stay just for a while until I could get some money saved up to get my own place. As I walked, I said that prayer.

After that I stopped over at a friend's house. I said I was just visiting and was too tired to go home. I was invited to stay over because it was too late to be traveling. I was so happy to hear that because I had nowhere to go. I went upstairs and got right into bed. It felt so cozy not to have a worry on my mind. As soon as my head hit the pillow, I was out. I slept like a baby. The next day I felt stress-free, and I even had breakfast in bed. No one had ever fixed me breakfast in bed, so I'm thinking maybe they knew what was happening to me and that's why they were being so nice.

In the meantime I was still closed by so I cloud go around the corner to visit my kids. For months, my kids and I were living in separate houses.

Just when I thought things were going well, here comes Jeffrey, making up more lies to tell me about how he *really* got himself together and how this time he's going to make it work. I was so tired of living like that and didn't care any longer about his lying words. I was done with the running back and forth. It was all too much for me. His stealing my money was the end of the road. I was just tired of living that way.

Sometimes we had gone to other people's houses when he thought they were cooking, just so we could eat every day. We lived like homeless people because of his drug use. I hated those nights when I had to hear my babies cry because they had no more milk. Instead we gave them sugar water in a bottle to make them stop crying. Many nights we didn't have anything. The best decision I had made in my life up to that time was to pack my stuff and leave that man's sorry behind. I didn't have the slightest idea of what life lay ahead for me. But I kept moving and didn't look back.

I was free and had no worries. There was no one to steal my money, and I could buy things for my children. But after all Jeffrey did to me, I still loved him. What kept me from going back was that after I had my son, Jeffrey took everything that I had. It was horrible. I couldn't have visitors. My blood pressure was up so high that I was put in ICU for two days. I wasn't allowed to see my son after he was born. Everyone else came to see my first baby boy, but I couldn't. I was the only one who didn't get to hold him on his first day of life.

After all that, I started going to church. I also started looking for jobs and saving my money to get my own place. I had moved to a whole different area just so I would be close to my family. I went back to school and tried to get my life in order. I spent a lot of time with my family at their friend's house because that's where everything happened.

It was the hangout spot. I had fun like any other teenager, and I met some new friends. I was a teenager with four kids, but I was free to do whatever I wanted to.

It felt good not having someone to tell me what to do and when to do it. It felt good to be able to buy my kids new things when I got money. The smiles on their faces were priceless. My girls were very happy when we went shoe shopping. It was wonderful to me because I really didn't know how much they had been missing.

As time passed, I got into another relationship with a new guy who was supposed to be just a friend. My friends constantly told me how nice he was and how he was always talking about me to them. So I told them to pass my phone number on to him. Every time I was around, I would hear how well this guy could sing. I never looked at him in any other way until one day he called me and started singing to me on the phone. Right then I was in love all over again. It was easy for me to fall in love with him—I had never heard a voice like his before.

I never knew that a man could be so in touch with his feelings. We talked every night and we hung out every day. I tried to keep my feelings inside. I didn't want him to know that I was falling for him so fast. The time we spent together we opened up to each other. We were very comfortable about telling our life stories and secrets. I told him everything about my troubles with my ex-boyfriend and the reason I didn't want to be in a relationship.

Finally, at the age of twenty-one, I moved into my own house with the help of my mother Mickey. It was a three-bedroom house with a porch, bathroom, living room, dining room, and a huge kitchen with a backyard. My kids and I were so happy that when we went to the new house on the first night, we stayed there with no beds and slept on the floor with blankets. We decorated the house the best we could and got by with what we needed. I had to stop buying clothes for the kids all the time as I had been. Paying my bills came first, and I recognized that it was essential to take care of other important things like Pampers, food, and baby milk.

We finally got things together with the house. At this time I got an unusual phone call from my sister Jazz, asking if she could come live with me. My answer was yes, because I needed someone to help me pay the bills anyway. We all agreed that there would be no men allowed to move into this house. We made the rules—and then we all broke them. Three women were sharing a home with seven children, and all was well. Allowing my sister to move in with us was a good decision. She helped pay the bills.

We started entertaining people such as male friends we already knew. *Here I go again*, I thought. I started to fall in love, and Terrace never missed a day coming over. Most of the time he would spend the night. After a while he came by himself and didn't care whether my sister's friend was there or not. When he came over, we would talk a lot and take the children to the park or just around the block. I thought this man was a real family person and imagined spending my life with him, as he would be a good stepfather to my children.

As we spent time together, we grew closer and closer. He had kids who were about the same age as my youngest child. We introduced our children and let them play together and get better acquainted. As we started to build our relationship, he asked if he could move in with me. I told him no. I really didn't want a man living with me. I also told him that we had an agreement not to let any men move in with us. He then explained to me that he had had an argument with the person he was staying with, who asked him to leave the house.

I allowed him to spend the night, and told him I would talk to the other women who lived at the house with me. Maybe they would allow him to stay with us. He tried to persuade me by saying that he would help pay bills and rent and buy food, as well as help with other things around the house.

I thought he was going to be a good help to all of us, so the next day when he went to get his belongings, I had a talk with the women who lived with me, trying to convince them to let Terrace move in. They finally said yes, and that's when things changed. After that, everybody's boyfriend started moving in without even asking.

I remember Terrace running around the house, playing with the other women. Sometimes when I went to bed, Terrace would sneak downstairs to be with Mickey. The thought of them trying to be together never entered my mind. What child would think such a thing? And besides, I was pregnant again. I remember having to get up to use the bathroom a few nights, and when I got up I could hear them downstairs, talking and laughing.

One day I sat at the top of the stairs for a while just to hear what they were talking about. I didn't get to hear much because they were very quiet, and it seemed they knew I was listening. I was determined to find out what was going on, so I faked pain and went downstairs to see what was going on. When I walked into the kitchen, Terrace was waiting for food he was cooking, and Mickey was warming food for her boyfriend—or so it seemed. They looked guilty, and both of them asked if I was in labor. I looked around to see if anything was out of place. Everything seemed to look okay. I told them I wasn't in labor and just needed something to drink. After I got my cup of water, I asked Terrace if he was coming to bed. He had a confused look on his face and said he didn't know. He finally said he would after his food was done.

When I went back upstairs, it was difficult for me to go to sleep. The baby was positioned in a knot in one spot and wouldn't move. My heart pounded as if I had run ten laps around a race track, and I couldn't calm down. I even tried taking deep breaths, but that didn't help at all. It seemed like Terrace was taking too long to come to bed, so I went downstairs and began to watch television. Terrace came in the living room with me and sat on the couch across the room. He asked if I was okay and if I was ready for him to come to bed. I just looked at him and smiled.

Days later, there were times when I would hear Jazz and my mother, Mickey, talking about current events regarding the house. They spoke about topics I didn't want to know about. One day Mickey came to me and told me that Terrace needed to leave because he wasn't helping out the way he should. I grew suspicious and asked Terrace myself what was going on. I told him that he needed to help out around the house if he wanted to continue to live there. He got very upset, grew angry with me, and said he wasn't going anywhere. and if Mickey wanted him to leave she would have to put him out. I looked at him as if he was crazy for disrespecting Mickey—she had been nice enough to allow him to stay with us. We discussed what he could do to be more helpful around the house, and he agreed to start putting out the trash just to make Mickey happy. But it still didn't stop her from holding meetings with the others about me.

Months and years passed, but the playing between Terrace and Mickey didn't, nor did the secret meetings stop. I always wondered why

Terrace never wanted to join me in any outdoor activities. He would always suggest staying home with Mickey while they watched the kids. Mickey had a habit of saying she would watch Jazz kids, and Terrace would watch mine. I was about seven or eight months pregnant with our first child. Every time Jazz and I took a walk, I told her that I thought something was going on between Mickey and Terrace. Jazz would look at me as if she wanted to tell me something but couldn't.

I prayed and asked God to help me with my jealousy because each time I saw Mickey and Terrace playing, it made me upset, even when he did it jokingly. I can't explain why I was so jealous, but the feeling was strong. Seeing Mickey, someone I looked up to as a mother, running around the house with Terrace like they were kids really bothered me. It was nerve-racking. I was kind of glad Terrace got locked up for past warrants. I went to the prison—big belly and all—to visit him faithfully.

I went into labor after he had been home for about a month. My second son was born on Mickey's birthday. She was happy her grandson was born on her birthday. I was happy because that started a new chapter of my life. Terrace was so happy he came home to celebrate with friends. I stayed in the hospital for two days while Mickey took care of my other children. However, when I came home from the hospital, the same activity with Mickey and Terrace continued.

One day Jazz told me what went on while I was in the hospital. She told me she suspected that something was going on with Mickey and Terrace. It was difficult for her to just spell it out and tell me. Oh, I *tried* to get it out of her, but Jazz didn't want to accuse Mickey and Terrace because she didn't want to be wrong about what she thought. I confronted Terrace and told him that I needed to know what was going on between him and Mickey. Mickey and I argued all the time and for no reason. I told Terrace that it was time for us to move because I couldn't stand the suspicion I had.

We moved into an apartment. This place was dilapidated and not fit for my family. Some people Terrace had known owned a building and collected rent for the place. If the tenants did not pay rent, they were given notice to leave. In my opinion, the entire building needed to be knocked down because there were no bathrooms, running water, or heat. There were no toilets. We used a Porta-Potty. We had to cook food on hot plates. Our rent was $350 a month. The one-room apartment needed work, and Terrace did the best he could to make it habitable for us. I was just happy to have our own place and not have to hear Mickey complain anymore about how much she didn't want Terrace living with us. The apartment had a back room, which I made suitable for my five children. They were all too young to remember later what was going on.

My friend began to sell drugs to make ends meet. He sold to everyone in the building. This was something I had to get used to because I didn't want to go back to living with Mickey and Jazz. I felt they were against me anyway, so I stuck it out where I was. I was afraid for my life and my children's lives every night.

One night we went out for a couple of hours. When we came back, people were saying some guys came into the building with guns, trying to rob the place and asking where the drugs were. But at that time there weren't any because they had just sold out. They even searched the house for money. They did get about a hundred dollars. That was the only thing they could find. Terrace wasn't worried because as long as they didn't get into our place, he was okay.

CHAPTER THREE

Terrace asked whether anyone had a description of these guys because he wanted to retaliate for them coming up in the building and trying to rob him. All I could do was hope that none of the people remembered who they were or what they looked like. I just wanted to keep all of the dangers of gangbanging away from my family. It took a lot for me to talk Terrace out of retaliating, but nothing I said mattered to him. He wanted revenge. He went so far as calling up all his friends to get a weapon. To safeguard the lives of my children, I prayed and asked God to watch over him while he went out looking for the people who robbed the building.

Meanwhile, he told me to lock the doors and not sell anything to anyone. Hours and hours passed. All that kept running through my head was that something might have happened. No one called to say whether they were okay. Later on I heard someone outside talking. Then I heard Terrace's voice saying how they looked all over and couldn't find the guys who robbed the place. I was happy to see him. It was getting late, and I thought that someone might have been really hurt. The guys with Terrace were talking about how other people said that they knew who those boys are that robbed the place. They said that they were going to look out for them.

Months had passed after the robbery. Everybody in the apartment agreed: since the stick-up boys were still on the loose, we had to lock the doors at a decent time and not let anyone in. But that didn't work. One night Terrace was sick, and he took something that made him sleepy. At first he was sitting outside on the steps, selling to whoever came up, but it started getting cold outside, so he came in the house.

I was scared, so I didn't want him to forget about locking the door. But every time I told him to get up and go lock the front door, he wouldn't because he said he was going back out on the steps. I just left it alone, and we sat up watching TV for a few minutes.

Then I went to sleep. I had just finished putting my baby to sleep. As soon as I got comfortably asleep, I thought that I was dreaming. In my dream we were getting busted by the police. We *were* getting busted for real—but not by the police. We were being robbed again by the stick-up boys, all because Terrace didn't lock the door.

In the meantime, I was lying down on this long couch with my baby, and I heard a loud noise. So I looked up, and there were the boys standing over Terrace. I thought he was shot because I heard the gun go off, but I didn't see any blood. I just started crying, telling the boys, "Please don't kill me because I have my baby here!"

But they didn't care about that. They put the gun to my head while I had my son lying next to me, and they told me to shut the f*** up or they would kill me. I was sure I was going to die with my baby beside me. They still were looking for drugs and money. That night they took everything. I didn't care because we still had our lives. That's all that mattered to me.

That gun was so loud that it could have awakened the other kids in the next room. But by the grace of God, my kids' lives were spared. All it would have taken was for one of them to come out of that room when the boys were there, and they would have gotten shot because the boys were already rushing and scared.

After that day, I went around the corner to use the pay phone. I called Mickey to ask if I could come back home. I started telling her what happened to me and how unsafe I felt there in that apartment with the drug-selling, robbing, and insecurity. She didn't care. She told me no. My babies and I could not come back there. She didn't want anyone living with her anymore.

So I told her she shouldn't let anything or anyone come between us. If something happened to me or my babies, she would feel bad about it. But that didn't change anything. The answer was still no. She said she would say a prayer for us and things would be okay. I was so upset that I didn't care whether she prayed or not, because she really didn't give a crap!

I had no choice but to stay where I was with my kids. I was so hurt that the woman who gave me life would turn her back on me as she did, knowing we were in a dangerous situation. I cried every night, too scared to close my eyes because that's all I could remember when those boys had that gun to my head telling me to shut up.

I just had to do something to get myself and my children out of that situation. Every time Terrace left the house, I would sell his stuff and put away the money that I made. He would count his stuff and always noticed that some of it was missing. I felt bad taking away from him. Each time I did, he had to work twice as hard to get the money back. He knew how uncomfortable I was living there with my children, so we talked about moving, and he agreed to give me money to move into any house I could find.

I looked in the newspaper every day, walked around the neighborhood, and asked people for references to landlords. I had no luck until finally I asked a friend if she could put in a good word with a person she knows. Within a couple of days I received a phone call about a house. The landlord said he would be showing the house the next day. I was happy because anything was better than living in a drug house with my babies. That day Terrace gave me money with no problem. He was ready to move, too.

Shortly thereafter, we moved into our second new home. When I first walked in, I saw that it needed a lot of love such as touch-ups, but it wasn't anything that we couldn't fix. We had our own little space to raise our family the right way, but I didn't know there were more hills to climb down the road.

Everything seemed to be so perfect in this house. It was my oldest child's first day of school, and we both were so happy. I remember taking her to school on her first day. She had no idea that I was going to leave her there, so when she was dropped off she would cry. She got used to it quickly, and every day she had a story to tell about what went on in school. She was only six years old when things about her began to change. I didn't realize it until the teacher brought to my attention that she had become very quiet and withdrawn.

To me, she seemed fine. At home she played with her siblings like any other kid. She was always a little more reserved than my others, and that's why I didn't think anything was wrong. I began to notice a change in my daughter over the years. She went from a joyful, talkative little girl to a child who spoke less and less.

She had such a depressed discontentment about her that her teachers became very concerned and suggested she see a doctor.

It got to the point that every time I picked her up from school, the counselor would pull me aside and ask if everything was okay at home. I would of course say yes, because I was rarely at home. I worked two jobs trying to make ends meet. At that time, I didn't know how important it was for me to be present for my children. My six-year-old daughter was my babysitter because I could not afford one. I trusted her to follow the rules, and she was very good at doing what I told her to do. She never opened the door for anyone, not even for my own relatives.

She tried cooking using the microwave because she knew not to touch the oven when I was not around. Sometimes on the weekends, if there was time, I would make dinner for them to eat before going to work. In the meantime, Terrace got laid off his job and started staying home with the kids while I worked. He started cooking all the meals and cleaning the house, and he made sure the kids had baths and were ready for school the next day. I thought he was the best person ever to look after the kids while I was working so hard.

CHAPTER FOUR

My dreams quickly came to an end. I felt like someone had sucked all the air out of my body. One day out of the blue, Terrace told me he went to my old house, the place I left because there where too many women under one roof. His reason for going back was to pick up some clothes and things that he left when we moved out.

He told me that Mickey wouldn't open the door for him because she didn't want him there. I wanted to talk to her to set her straight so he could get his things. Then, the next time he made that trip, there wouldn't be a problem between the two of them. We didn't have a phone at the time, because we just moved in our new house. Terrace left a few weeks later to attempt to go back and get the rest of his stuff. He started telling me about the argument he and Mickey had. Something didn't seem right, so I went to use the phone at the corner by my house to hear Mickey side of the story.

I was on the phone, asking her what happened, and she said that she didn't want Terrace there because he was trying to seduce her. I couldn't believe what she was telling me! She told me that they had been having sex since I was pregnant with our first child. She indicated that he didn't want to go to the streets for sex because he didn't want to bring me back any STD, so he had it with her. They had been intimate for some time. It was going on even while I was in the hospital giving birth.

While she was talking to me, telling all of her nasty little secrets, I felt as if my soul was gone. I couldn't bear to hear anything more she had to say about the two of them, but she continued with the story. She told me that she was not the only person he had been trying to seduce in the house. There was another woman involved. When I asked who the other person was, Mickey told me it was someone very close to me, but she wouldn't give a name. Right there and then I knew that the other person was Jazz.

I was extremely hurt that day, thinking that God couldn't take this pain away from me. I lost two important people to this freak! I cared a lot about this man. What was the problem? I wasn't enough for him? I don't even know why I wanted all the details of where they had sex, and how often they had it, or what acts were performed. I got so angry that I started banging the phone against the booth. I just couldn't believe what I was hearing. That day I called all around just to find out who the other person was in this sick, nasty love game that they had going on without me knowing. Finally, after a few weeks had passed, I got in touch with the other woman who was Jazz that played a part in this. She confirmed the whole story. She told me he performed oral sex on her a couple of times. But from what I knew already, she was telling me a lie. It happened more than twice.

So I got upset with her because she was denying everything. I asked to speak with her friend so that he could know what was going on. While I was on the phone with him, I heard Terrace's voice in the background. When I asked to speak with him, I heard Terrace screaming as he was running down his friend's stairs because he knew that I had found out what was going on with him all these years.

I cried all the way home. I couldn't look at my own baby, knowing what Terrace done. I didn't want anything to do with him any more because I hated him. I lost all of my self-esteem. I felt ugly and thought about committing suicide. How could he tell me I was beautiful when he had sex with all these other women?

I wanted everything to go away. That's when I decided to give up my child just until I could get myself together. I couldn't love him as a mother should. I had a lot of self-hate in me. I wanted to commit suicide so badly that I sat at the table with all the lights in the house off and a knife at my side.

My other four children stayed with a family member as well, because nobody trusted me as depressed as I was. I needed peace but couldn't find it. I needed time to think about what to do and say when Terrace came walking through those doors.

When he did come home finally, he stopped at the front door and saw his bags were packed and ready to go. He didn't need to step any further into my house. He begged me to talk to him and asked for forgiveness. I was too distraught to speak.

He tried to explain that he thought if he discontinued his affair with these women, we would have been homeless. The woman he had the affair with begged him to leave me for her. But nothing he said to me was the truth, not one word. All the while I could think only about their affair. It was only God that kept me from stabbing him. *He* kept me calm at the table. Praying for my heart to be healed and to control my anger, I lifted my head and commanded Terrace to get out and never come back.

He still tried to make me understand why he did what he did. That's when I took the knife and threw it at him. I wanted him out my house! I didn't care whether he was homeless or had a place to lay his head. It took a long time before I could visit my family and get my babies back. I tortured myself every day. My heart was so full of hate that I couldn't eat. I couldn't pray because I didn't know what to pray for anymore. My family was not a family anymore. Why did God allow this to happen to me? I guess that's something I will never know.

I had thought everything was on track with my life and my family. Now I stayed home all the time with the lights off because that's what I felt inside: total darkness. I wouldn't answer the phone when people called, nor would I open the door for visitors. I became an empty shell, hiding from the world and unable to do anything to make myself feel better. I cried, starved myself, lost a lot of weight, and became weaker and weaker from not eating.

One day the phone rang. Something kept telling me to pick up the phone. It took some time to get to the phone because I was very weak. But before I could answer, the phone stopped ringing.

I lay across the couch in case the person called back. Finally, just as I was about to get up and go upstairs to my room, the phone rang again. It was my grandmother. To me she always had the sweetest voice, the kind of voice that soothes even the most depressed person. We started talking about everything that happened, and she said something profound. She told me no matter what happened to me, I needed to forgive because if I didn't, God would hold me accountable for it.

At the time, I wasn't sure what she meant by that, but the Bible says that if you judge someone, you will be judged the same way when Judgment Day comes. I started thinking about my life and all the not-so-good things that I did in the past. I didn't want God to hold any of those things against me. I wanted to be forgiven.

CHAPTER FIVE

Every morning I read the Bible. The chapters that most held my attention were 1 Peter 4 and Matthew 5:7–9. Every day I grew stronger and stronger until I was able to get out of bed, put on clothes, and do my hair. I even started to eat small portions of food. Every day I listened to gospel songs, and they began to breathe new life into my soul.

I found myself crying tears of joy. I was able to move on after that test. The Devil wanted me to go on a killing spree or perhaps commit suicide. But God stepped in and did not let Satan take me, God's child. There is something God wants me to do and I can't die until it's finished. It's all in the will of God; it's in his hands.

As time passed, I was able to call the woman who had the affair with Terrace. I told her that I love her and apologized for saying hateful things to her. I told her that I missed her and invited her to my house for Sunday dinner. She was so happy when she got that phone call from me. I heard joy in her voice. She began to cry and apologized to me. She told me that she missed me too and that she was sorry anything like that had ever happened. As I patched things up I could feel the healing begin. I started enjoying other people's company just as if nothing ever happened.

And I finally got my children back. I'd thought I lost my motherly connection with them, but my love for my children was too strong. It was wonderful to hold my baby in my arms again and to hear that word *Mommy* that warmed my heart every time. Life started to have new meaning to me again. All my children were back together. I was healing from that terrible incident.

Through it all, I learned how to love myself all over again. I would constantly hear how beautiful I was, but I never really felt beautiful inside or out. It was hard to see myself as a beautiful person. It didn't matter how much weight I gained or lost. I still had the same face and emotional problems.

I took Terrace back after everything he had done, not knowing why—I just did. In part, I didn't know how to confront emotional issues but was looking to get off to a fresh start. I asked myself a lot of questions about what went wrong between us. He didn't know why he had affairs with any of those women. His answers always hurt me, but for some reason I thought that after being apart for a couple of years, I would be able to understand his side of the story.

After all those years, the hurt I felt on the day I found out he had the affairs was still there as if it happened yesterday. My soul had not been right since then even though I prayed and asked God to help me to be able to love others. But I had lost trust in everybody. There was no one I could trust, even if they said they were trustworthy. It took a lot of Bible reading, and even then I was not complete because I couldn't understand what I read in God's book of life. But what I did know was that the Bible talks about what love is and how it is supposed to feel.

Right then and there I wanted to know what love feels like. And what better place to find it than in God's Word? At this time of my life, I took whatever came my way. If I accepted someone who did me so wrong back into my life, it was because I thought nothing of myself. I accepted that I did not deserve better than what he had to offer me.

Shortly thereafter, I found out that I was three months pregnant again. Since I didn't want to chase Terrace away again, I hid the pregnancy and got an abortion a few days form mothers day. It seemed as if I owed him something, even though I was the victim in this relationship.

Terrace had the audacity to make me think I did something wrong to him. I guess that is what happens when you allow someone back into your life who did nothing but treat you like crap from the beginning of your relationship.

The next day I was told that Terrace wasn't the one who came to pick me up from the hospital. It was a family member. I got no flowers, cards, or gifts from Terrace at all. My self-esteem was so low that staying with Terrace was all I could do at the time. I thought no one else would ever see what he saw in me—which was nothing.

I was the mother of five children. I wondered who would want me now. Terrace had me right where he wanted me, and I was right where I thought I should be. He told me that I was fat and needed to lose weight. He tried to change me to be who he wanted me to be because he was not happy with who he was.

No matter what happened, though, I kept my job. Going to work was the only way I could relieve some of my depression and stay away from home. Being home made me depressed. I felt nothing but total darkness on the inside when I was at home all the time. That cold, dark spirit would not lift.

It seemed like everybody who lived in this home was depressed. So some mornings when Terrace took a walk, I would get up and anoint all the doors in the house and then myself and my kids to lift that cold dark spirit that was always around.

Deep down inside I knew something wasn't right, but I didn't know what. Something was going on in that house that I could not figure out.

My kids were always happy to see me come home from work. They would all crawl into my bed or sometimes camp out on the floor just to be near me. They were happy to be out of harm's way. I built what I thought was a tight relationship with my children. I would spend time alone with them just to talk to see what their day was like. I would tell them, "No matter what you have to tell me, say it anyway."

I wanted them to feel comfortable telling me anything. So I assured them I would protect them and take care of them even if it meant my own life.

From that point, they started to open up, saying what was on their little minds. They would sometimes start off saying crazy things, but I would still listen. Most of the time, we would have fun conversations just to make each other laugh. My youngest did most of the talking while the others just listened and laughed.

One day we had to have a serious conversation about people touching others where they don't want to be touched. So I asked questions about whether anyone had ever touched them in a place where they felt uncomfortable.

They all looked at each other smiling and saying nobody ever touched them like that. I had to make sure they were being honest, so I asked them again, and one of the kids said the physician did. Upon asking what the physician did, my child said the physician did eye and ear checks. So I had to tell them what I meant by asking them that serious question. I asked them if anyone had ever touched their private parts. I encouraged them to let me know if a situation like that ever happens.

Summer came. The kids were out of school. They would sometimes stay at home or play with the other children outside where we lived. One day it was so nice outside that I decided to get off work early just so I could spend some time with my children.

Coming from work, I happened to see all my kids playing outside except one. I was told Terrace picked up the youngest and took her home. When I asked why was she the only one at home, he said the room needed to be cleaned.

I wondered why Terrace didn't take the other kids with him. So of course my mind started generating all kinds of bad thoughts. I had to pray and ask God to give me a clear mind because I didn't want to think something bad had happened if it didn't. As I walked though the house after asking Terrace questions and going up the steps, I saw in my kid's room just a little bit. The room door was crack opened.

From where I was, until I opened the room door, it looked like nobody was in the room. But my daughter was sitting in the room, putting dirty clothes in the basket.

A day later I thought it would be okay to ask my child the same question that I asked Terrace. He asked me if I could help find his shirt. She also told me he paid her for helping him. As she told me what happened, I sensed in my heart that something was not right.

I sat her down and began to ask more questions about how much money he gave her. She told me he gave her twenty dollars. That's when I knew something wasn't right. He's so tight when it comes down to his money. He doesn't give it away for nothing.

CHAPTER SIX

I refreshed our conversation about unclean touching, and she remembered all we discussed. There was no time during the conversation that she mentioned anything about sexual touching. Things began to look more and more out of place. Being a young mother was hard, but there were three things that I always kept up with: my kids' appointments, getting them to school, and going to work.

One morning while getting my daughter ready for school, she started complaining about her vagina. I started asking her questions, but she was too young to explain how she was feeling. So that very day I rushed her to the emergency room. She was only seven years old, so I knew it couldn't be a sexually transmitted disease. But as a mother, I was worried.

I didn't know what was going on with my child, but I sensed that it had to be something terrible. As I walked back into the room where my child was, people began to talk to me about her condition.

They informed me that it didn't seem like there were any sexual activities going on with her because everything was still intact. She was still a virgin, thank God. The irritation was coming from too many bubble baths.

I was so glad that was over. My heart was pounding hard while these people checked my child. I wouldn't know where to start if I had to tell them Terrace sexually molested her. How would a mother bring herself to say anything like that?

After all that, Terrace knew he had to get the attention off of himself so he could keep doing whatever he wanted to do with the girls. It was a shame because he knew how to make the kids lie for him just to cover up the nasty things he would do to them. For a long time I was in the dark and didn't know anything was ever going on. I began to feel like a stranger in my own home. My children weren't holding conversations with me any more, even at times he wasn't around. It was like they had put up a barrier, trying to protect me from the painful news. He was a sick individual.

He played kiddy games with them like hide and seek with the lights off. He used to make the girls dance for him like in an exotic bar. They would stand on the dresser, and he would put money in their underwear.

There were times I came home from work and found my lingerie on the floor. Of course Terrace would lie when I asked him what happened during the day. He actually thought ten-, nine-, and eight-year-olds could satisfy him sexually. How could I not have known this sooner?

My oldest child began to shut down from everything that a young child should be doing. She was dealing with adult issues at the age of ten. Terrace tried to get a big thing going by asking my ten-year-old to invite some more girls over to our house. Out of embarrassment, she stopped talking to all of her friends and isolated herself. She didn't want anyone to talk about her and what was going on while I was at work. I couldn't wake up from this nightmare.

My self-esteem was at an all-time low. I was so stressed mentally that on some days I didn't think I would be able to make it from day to day. I decided to move again—without a man in my life. I felt good about the move. Somehow Terrace got locked up. I know I'm not supposed to take joy in others' misery, but I was happy. There was joy in knowing that they finally put him where he belongs.

We stayed with some strangers for three months until the house was ready. My ten-year-old child graduated from sixth grade, and looking at her on graduation day, she seemed fine. She contained her feelings very well. Little did I know she was hiding deep, dark secrets that I believe she had been carrying for a long time.

I was proud of her because her name was called many times for awards during graduation. God blessed her and gave her strength to make it. She was rewarded with $950 in savings bonds for high achievement. This was the best day of both of our lives. She accomplished a great deal after everything she went through.

Moving was like a fresh start for me and safe ground for my children. But my child could not forget what happened to her. She had a nervous breakdown and tried to commit suicide by cutting her wrists.

I rushed her to the hospital. As I was waiting in the waiting area at the emergency room, all I could think of was that I should be in her place.

People called to speak with me, but I was not in my right mind. I couldn't believe what they told me about what had been done to her. To keep her silent, Terrace had threatened to kill me if she ever told anyone. I was the only parent my children had. So she felt she had to protect me.

He used the girls as strippers and took their purity from them. He made them dress up in my lingerie, making them think it was for fun and games. He played with their little breasts and made them think everything he was doing to them was okay by giving them money. He made them challenge each other to see who the best dancer was and who would earn the most money. He used his hands to touch them in places he was not supposed to, then he would tell them to lie down so that he could perform sexual acts with them. How disgusting!

He told them that what he was doing would not hurt them. I can imagine their little hearts racing and them being so afraid that they could not breathe from being overwhelmed with the pressure and pain! He took their virginity, and while he was doing that, he would tell them to be quiet as he hurt them.

They respected him as a father, but he was a monster who preys on little girls, waiting for them to get a little older. I tried not to think of the times I used to get them out of the tub and tell them to run to my room so that I could dry them off. When he was in that room, it never occurred to me that he would think of touching them in any manner. He was supposed to be the person they run to when someone was trying to harm them.

CHAPTER SEVEN

Satan tried to destroy my family. He tried to destroy me in so many ways, even through death by suicide. Satan even tried to make me believe that everything that happened was my fault. One Sunday I decided to go to church. Out of nowhere a lady came up to me and offered me her number.

This woman became a mentor to me. She was a very good listener, and she kept me from making costly mistakes. I actually wanted to kill Terrace for what he had done. I thank God for bringing my mentor into my life. Despite my feeling of shame, I told her what had happened.

She prayed with me on the phone and gave me scriptures to read for strength. I received the prayer and read the scriptures, but it didn't matter because hatred remained in my heart for a long time. Again I was told not to hold hatred in my heart when I'm praying to God because my prayers would not be heard. That was all I needed to hear. I never want God to turn his back on me because of something that I could have talked to him about.

But in my mind I thought the Lord didn't care about anything I went through or was going through. It's terrible to be full of life and feel like you're a walking dead person. It felt like there was no life in me at all; I was just here. Some days I would place my hand on my chest just to see if my heart was still beating.

There were times when I was in church and the pastor would make an altar call for those who were backsliders. I could not move or open my mouth to repent. I thought I would be in this state of mind forever. I remember talking to the Lord, saying that I was sorry for not opening my heart to him. That day I repented for my sins. I said the sinner's prayer, but my heart was still hardened against God.

I guess God knew that I was not sincere when I prayed. I had to believe God would fix the things that were broken in my life. So not only did I have to pray, I also began to study the Word of God. I read every chapter that had to do with love and how to love my enemies.

My ex-boyfriend had the nerve to call me collect. He wanted to talk. About what? I don't know. There were no reasons for me to hold any conversation with him. But that day I accepted his call. I asked him to just listen to me. I started reading from Psalm 23 ("The Lord is my shepherd"). Reading to him was my way of breaking free of all the things he had done to me.

I needed to let him know that I forgave him for what he had done to me and everyone I love. I told him to ask God to forgive him because I couldn't do it for him. He then quoted the sinner's prayer at my prompting and repented to God with the last minutes he had left on the phone. That was the last time I ever spoke with him.

By the grace of God, who is wonderful and merciful to us, he put angels around us and pulled us out of the stuff we thought that was never going to end—those nights the girls would wake up crying because they had nightmares about their abuser, the days when their thoughts were suicidal, when my house carried a dark cloud over it.

I had felt hate for everyone, even myself. I didn't feel worthy of the air God gave us. I was too depressed to appreciate all the wonderful things God had already done.

As time passes, my family grows stronger and closer together. My girls are all grown up with their high school diplomas. Some of them went on to trade schools after graduating so they could have better careers.

I could go on and on talking about how Satan tried to kill me and my children. Glory be to God, for when God steps in, there is no room for the Devil. I am blessed and gifted by God that everything I went through was for a reason.

God knew what was going to happen before it happened, and I wouldn't change a thing. I have wanted to question God about my life, but I never had time to say anything. Somehow I would get so busy when things happened. I would just ask him to help me go through whatever it was and to make me strong for whatever he needs me to do.

Through it all, there was never a time I asked God, *Why me?* Never did those words come out my mouth. I learned the hard way that it wasn't always about me, and I had to bow down to worship and praise God through it all.

During both good times and bad, God deserves to be praised. We never really want to do anything until we see changes happening in our life. Then our faith kicks in because we can *see* it. It wasn't until I started believing in what I was praying for that things started to change. I asked God to help me with my ego, which was too big for my own good.

The Bible says every knee shall bow. Until you break the stronghold of Satan, nothing will happen. During my time of trouble, I didn't realize all I needed to do was just open my mouth and ask God for help. At the same time, I had to build up faith to believe that whatever I ask him for he will supply.

After all my children and I had gone through, my faith had been at an-all time low. Trust for anybody was out the door, even after I started going to church. The pastor's words never seemed to mean anything to me because it was all still coming from another man. Then I opened the Holy Bible and saw that the Word this man was speaking came from a far more powerful place. That's when reading the Bible took its place in my life.

Because I had been deceived by many, there was nothing anybody could just tell me. I had to see it for myself. As I begin to grow spiritually, my understanding of the Word of God became clear. Changes were happening. Chains began to break. There were no more restless nights for me or my children.

Day by day I saw them begin to heal. There was no more going in and out of mental hospitals. I could tell my kids were feeling safe again. They no longer woke up crying from nightmares that intruded on life's daily activities such as playing with other children or being around people other than me. During the dark times, I was the only one they would trust. Even then, at times they would shut down on me out of fear.

As time passed, my children wanted to see Terrace face-to-face. They had never been able to confront him. They were still afraid of him, but they wanted him to see that nothing he did to them had broken them. Thank God, they were able to move on with life without the stranglehold of Satan, even though for many years they were molested, and for many years they had attempted suicide.

Negative thoughts were all they knew. But the Bible tells us to cast all troubles upon God, for he will give you peace. We started to have prayer circles in our home. I would have my children hold hands, and each of them would have a turn to speak to God. I kept that going until I felt they were strong enough to pray on their own. Let me say it again: by the grace of God, who is wonderful and merciful to us, he put angels around us and pulled us out of the stuff we thought was never going to end.

I'm blessed. Through everything we endure, we learn to put God first and trust in his Word. We bring each other joy, and we help each other stay strong. It was a very long journey for my family, but thank God, we made it.

Just know that whatever God puts in your path, you can go through it. Don't try to do it alone. God alone is a strong tower. The righteous run to him and are safe.

Printed in the United States
By Bookmasters